Robert Hamberger

Blue Wallpaper

First published in 2019
by Waterloo Press (Hove)
95 Wick Hall
Furze Hill
Hove BN3 1NG

Printed in Palatino 11pt by
OneDigital
54 Hollingdean Road
East Sussex BN2 4AA

A CIP record for this book is available
from the British Library

ISBN: 978-1-906742-85-0

Acknowledgements

Acknowledgements are due to the editors of the following publications, in which some of these poems, including earlier versions, first appeared: *Acumen; Agenda; Ambit; Cake; Coffee House; Chroma; Divining Divas* (edited by Michael Montlack; Lethe Press, New Jersey); *The Echo Room; 14 Magazine; The Frogmore Papers; The Gibson Memorial Poetry Competition Anthology* (The Thomas Hardy Society, Dorchester); *Hand Luggage Only* (edited by Christopher Whitby, Open Poetry Ltd, Leicestershire); *The Harlequin; The Interpreter's House; Languages of Colour* (edited by Alexandra Loske, The Frogmore Press, East Sussex); *Litter; The London Magazine; Magma; Nimrod; The North; Obsessed With Pipework; The Poetry Review; The Rialto; The SHOp; Smiths Knoll; Stand* and *Under The Radar*.

Thanks are due to Gillie Bolton; Bernadette Cremin; Robert Dickinson; Hugh Dunkerley; Nell Farrell; Naomi Foyle; Mark Goodwin; Maria Jastrzebska; Joanna Lowry; John McCullough; Marian McCraith; Joan Poulson; Alicia Stubbersfield; Janet Sutherland; Jackie Wills; River Wolton and Gregory Woods for their support in improving these poems.

'Dancing in the street' includes lyrics by William "Mickey" Stevenson, Marvin Gaye and Ivy Jo Hunter (Jobete Music Inc, 1964). 'Mad about the boy' includes lyrics from 'Is you is or is you ain't my baby?' by Louis Jordan and Billy Austin, 1956. The epigraph to 'Twenty, thirty years' is from *The Waves* by Virginia Woolf (The Hogarth Press, Ltd, London 1931 Page 172). The epigraph to 'Failure, my horse' is from *A lesson from Michelangelo* by James Fenton, published in *The Strength of Poetry* (Oxford University Press, Oxford 2001 Page 5). The epigraph to 'The AIDS Memorial' is from *Just Kids* by Patti Smith (Bloomsbury Publishing Plc, London 2010 Page 287.) The poem includes a quotation from *Poems and Prose of Gerard Manley Hopkins* (Penguin Books Ltd, London 1985 Page 63.)

'In Justice Square' was third prizewinner in *Chroma's* International Queer Writing Competition, 2009.

Rimbaud variations are from literal translations by Keith Rainger. French texts are from *Arthur Rimbaud Collected Poems* (Oxford University Press, 2001). Heartfelt thanks are always due to Keith for being my husband, collaborator, first reader and constant friend.

Contents

Golden dragon

Husbands

Being the sea

for

Ava, Ithamar, Xalia and Freddie

The lesson of sand

My mother as Ingrid Bergman

Sometimes my mother blurs with Ingrid Bergman
in *Casablanca*. They share that same look:
proud profile; high-glossed hair; tilted chin
lit through dark blinds, while two lovers talk
about Paris and a song they'll play again.
It's her dazzle I love in photos:
my black-and-white mother before I was born,
with her sisters, her husband. The woman she was,
happy and glamorous, years of her life
ahead. When Ingrid faces the camera
for *Here's looking at you kid* she might stay safe
in his arms this time. At night my mother
stars in the last reel, soars to another country
through the fog, to freedom, over the sea.

Saying my name

My mother doesn't know me from Adam.
She's baffled by my face, wonders at my words.
I make no sense; but if I tell her who I am
my name might echo down her corridors
to a room where she sits by open windows,
looking up from empty hands to find me there.
She'll hear Robert because of course she knows
those syllables, familiar as a prayer.
It's worth a shot. I say it like a stone
dropped into her lake to test the water,
to see if bubbles ripple from my tone.
Nothing this time. I name my sons and daughter,
say her sisters' names, tell her all our news
to ease the silence, darkening like a bruise.

Not letting her know

She's outlived her sister and brother,
but hasn't been told. Letting her know
might twist the knife for no reason, a blow
to her belly from nowhere, another
useless fact. She'll live without the bother
of being reminded. Her hours flow
into each other: a pebbled stream where snow
melted last season, and she's no mother
or sister to anyone. She left
her past like clothes on a beach, found
herself miles away, safe in the cleft
of a rock beside the sea, its sound
easy as breathing, where sun's a gift
for her skin while she drowses on the sand.

The lesson of sand

My mother wouldn't visit her mother
in a home. She couldn't face it, face this:
an old woman staring, as if I'm glass
and she sees through me; her laughter
echoing mine like we're joking together,
though she can't speak a word or blow a kiss.
I'm greedy for more, not one minute less,
as she craved more than her mother could give her.
I stay for an hour, watching the lesson
of sand giving way again to sea.
When each visit ends it's hard to loosen
my fingers. I prise them gently
from her grip while she loses this man,
as if I run through her hands to be free.

Every visit

Though I'm bringing yellow chrysanthemums
at every visit a few more pounds
have gone. There's less of her to see; the sounds
she makes are softer. She yawns and seems
as weak and sleepy as a cat. Sometimes
I can reach her, but not now. A nurse stands
over us and explains the way her mind's
gone: *She lives in her senses now. Your mum's
smiles may only be a reflex. What kind
of woman was she? What music did she like?
Sinatra? I'll make a note. We'll find
a vase for those flowers.* His words take
their course, like water seeping through sand,
a babble for her dreams when she won't wake.

Mother's Day

You're a month dead and mothers are everywhere.
How can I avoid them? Walk to the sea.
Skirting the waves makes me too cold to care
about mothers or mourning, though I worry
where you are now, if you're safe from harm,
whether you've slipped your illness like a skin,
free from it at last, young again, arm in arm
with your sister, laughing, catching the sun.
I'd love it to be true. I sing your songs
to keep me company, choose a rose
today for the tide. Each gull-cry belongs
inside me. I'm dreading I might lose
your memory, remember less of you,
while the weeks and the waves continue.

Ash

Here's the message of ash: poured on water
it clouds into the lake, dissolving,
diminishing, until its plumes and waver
merge with maps across the sky, resolving
a reflection, the colour of weather,
while you become these voices in the park,
its laughter, squabbles, magnolias, lager,
its footballs, mongrels, whistles before dark,
that girl behind us weaving a daisy chain,
moorhens guarding their nests, all the mothers,
the couples, old women walking as if pain
slows them over the grass, three brothers
throwing their roses like ash onto this lake
where you're living now, where you'll always wake.

Coming home

Camel

Then my mother knitted a brown jumper
with a yellow camel across the chest.
Who else is here now to remember
this but me? I wore him with pride, the best
camel in class. No-one could miss me.
No other boy owned a yellow camel,
no girl either. Did a green palm tree
sway over my heart, that strange animal?
Did my camel once wink his brown wool eye?
In nine months I outgrew him. My father went
the way of camels and palm trees, and I
forgot my jumper when we were sent
packing to our new flat, where other
shapes filled the gap of a camel, a father.

Dancing in the street

That bass, those drums, her voice call me closer.
Are you ready for a brand new beat?
Two small horses drop onto the carpet
from my hands. I reach the room's bright corner
where our radiogram sings *Summer's here*
and the time is right for dancing in the street.
Gold mesh over the speaker hums like heat.
I kneel, press my ear against it, turn it louder
until drums, brass, chorus, tambourines
stroke my bones and stun my blood. I want
to live there *in Chicago, down in New Orleans,*
in New York City where the women chant
and stamp. *Turn it down!* my mother screams
as floorboards rattle, walls fall apart.

Serenade

Sound was the first I knew of him.
That almost wordless nasal moan
rose like a shadow of singing
up three floors.

It swelled our Sunday afternoon.
Held notes drew me outside.
I peered on tiptoe over
the landing wall to find him

serenading in the centre
of our flats, near the rusted
roundabout. This cloth-cap tenor
dragged his leg,

one sleeve of his khaki coat
pinned at the chest beside three medals;
his mouth like a dark glass raised to us
where music wavered.

Our mother doled out pennies,
a shilling, glint of half a crown.
We lobbed them over the edge
to wheel and spin and clatter by his boots.

Strawberry and lime

What flavours? She let us choose milkshakes.
We sat in Pellicci's, Bethnal Green Road:
my mother, my brother and me, well-fed
after lamb chops, finishing our drinks.
Two more turned up, as if our blinks
at empty glasses meant milkshakes flowed
from heaven. Nev Pellicci said:
He ordered them. We mumbled shy thanks
to a dark-haired man we'd never seen before.
He nodded from his table, and our mother
glanced at him again over my shoulder.
I sensed her secret thrill that he'd bother
to notice her. When I sucked my straw
pink bubbles popped, one after another.

The man in chains

A stone's throw from where Anne Boleyn lost
her head, the man in chains gathers a crowd.
We circle him, as he huffs and puffs his hard
bare chest. We hear his bellowed boast,
watch while a serious child tugs the last
padlock like a choker at his throat, proud
to prove him trapped: clinking links bound
around his torso; snake-tattoo arms crossed.
The fight begins. A struggle with himself.
Is this how much it costs to be a man?
He writhes and wrestles. We stare as if
he's smelting, metal loosening from his skin
like broken keys. He steps free. We pay him off.
Each coin spins the head of a silver queen.

My cousin Gillian

She shone in a ten-year old's gaze:
knew all the words
to *The Supremes Greatest Hits Volume One*,
those shimmering women in floaty gowns
who oohed and aahed about love
while she dolled herself up for the night.

Where was she going
as she sellotaped lacquered kiss-curls
against each cheek,
twisted a tiny sticky brush,
mascara'd her lashes to make them blacker,
smoothed lipstick pale as snowdrops
so her mouth looked chill?

I wanted to be as happy as her
while she prettied herself for the boys,
one of whom, the latest one,
might arrive in his mohair suit
with his tidy cut and clipped words,
loitering in the passage
suave as a cucumber, itching to leave.

I wanted to ride between them
on a scooter somewhere to darkness
where the beat brought them closer.
Who did I want to be if I wasn't me:
her or him; both or neither?

I might even dance past midnight,
feel someone cling to me
while they mouth the burning lines.
She taught the steps and I'm still learning
to be him or her, both or neither,
oohing and aahing about love.

Aunt Anna

We say her name. She high-heels through the room,
dripping with gold at her neck, lobes, wrists
and fingers, glittering the gloom.
Fish-nets at fifty, she whistles a taxi, persists
in leopard spots, tiger stripes, black skirt slashed
to her thigh. That time some bastard
mugged her, she grabbed a cosh from her bag, bashed
his head till he scarpered. She'd get plastered
at our parties, sing *All I want is a table*
and chair. I don't care, just a table and chair.
She'd kick her leg high and never topple,
shimmying way past the midnight hour,
dabbing her ash, sloshing another swig,
cramming her minutes with life, making them big.

Mr Muxworthy

In our last year before scattering
across ten secondary schools
and losing touch, we watched him
flirt with Miss Morris in assembly,
flicking his narrow tie and Welsh laughter.
He peeled off his shirt in front of us
that time before gym, baring his hairy chest,
its tangled fascination, elbowing himself
into maroon and yellow stripes,
ready to shout at us to run and run.

One afternoon he spoke about smoking,
lit a cigarette, sucked the filter slowly,
pouted his lips like a secret kiss.
The ashy tip glowed
its tiny cooling coal, singed from the heart.
He blew a mouthful of smoke
into his white handkerchief
and showed, at the centre,
a mustard rose spoiling the snow.

That's what it does to your lungs he said.
Could I crawl inside him,
tunnel to the trees barred by his ribcage,
stroke the smoky branches there,
gulp his danger back into my mouth?
The lilies of my lungs, clean as handkerchiefs,
ached to be tarred by him,
wanting to puff his confidence,
that cocksure laugh telling us all
It's time to go now. Hurry along.

Mad about the boy

After Dinah Washington

To hear a woman's voice as proud as this
lightens your loneliness. It won't solve it.
She doesn't expect it to. Love is bliss,
you bet, but it's a blasé *So what?*
a bare-shouldered shrug. Her raised eyebrow
tilts and swings the notes, steady as her range
above the strings, hearing the trumpets blow.
A man is a creature that's always been strange.
She's quite aware this earth may be bitter:
it crumbles in her throat like black bread.
Cool phrases swirl on her tongue, grittier
than sea-salt, lazier than a leopard.
Drunk on twenty songs as if they're wine
she opens her mouth, pours out the next line.

An interest in musicals

At *The Sound of Music* intermission
a smooth man approached near the choc-ices.
Blotched teenager, I gave him permission
to chat about his job, the cruises
and sunsets, while the citrus scent
he must have sprayed at his wrists and throat
flitted between us. I liked how he leant
when he laughed, showing his teeth, each note
of his voice gentle enough to draw me
closer. My mother arrived like a guard-dog
to shepherd me back in time for Julie
climbing every mountain. I couldn't beg
for a moment more. He left me songs
in the dark about my favourite things.

How to kiss

D'you want me to show you how to kiss?
I was sixteen and greedy to learn.
She was my brother's girlfriend under the moon,
standing outside a pub; the two of us
dry while he queued inside, oblivious.
It was worth the guilt. I stooped like a heron
to scoop a fish, as if breaking the skin
of water. She raised her throat, and this
moment banished feathers and scales. Her tongue
dipped briefly inside my mouth, the taste
of someone else, licked and gone.
My thumb stroked an inch of her wrist,
but my brother came barging out again
balancing bitter drinks to quench our thirst.

Lesson 2

A little less tongue. That's Patrick's advice.
I found him in the sauna, a white towel
draped over his loins; drowsy after a prowl
down dim-lit corridors where one man's face,
another man's torso, might entice.
He lazed alone inside the cubicle,
as if snoozing on an altar in a chapel,
until I hesitated, made my choice.
I stepped inside and he, by allowing me
to loosen his towel, strum the hairs on his thigh,
proved consent by the subtlest degree.
I'll do whatever Patrick tells me, try
a little less tongue tonight, softly
skim your lips with kisses where we lie.

Her husband

At seventeen in the Netherlands
I danced with my own dark lady, married
to a man who smoked all night, his hands
tapping his beer-glass, staring straight ahead,
while the music moved us closer.
She couldn't speak a word of English.
I knew no Dutch. He looked like a bruiser,
but I was flattered enough to blush
when she chose me for the next dance, and chose
again, through most of that night. Was I his
humiliation: the one she plucked as she rose
to each song, knowing he never danced, and this
foreign boy would? Back home, did he take
her face in his hands? Did they even speak?

Twenty, thirty years ago
for Clifford

No lullaby has ever occurred to me capable of singing him to rest.

Virginia Woolf
from *The Waves*

Talking tonight about his bitter death,
its pain, and how he hoped he'd never go,
where's the remedy? His name, that quick breath,
brings him back, standing by the window.
Once he said I was a brother to him.
Some people dance forever through your skin,
and twenty, thirty years ago we'd brim
with news, spilling our stories, two grown men
swapping silly voices, giggling like schoolgirls.
Once words ran out, we'd let ourselves be quiet,
as we stayed quiet for his drifts between pills
and sleep. I'd read to him, as I read his favourite
pages from *The Waves* when we were boys, believing
we'd ride against death, unvanquished, unyielding.

Coming home

A late sun slowly swerves behind the flats.
Foxes skulk between dustbins.
This playground empties like a name
called over and over to come home.
Windows paint lit squares against the black,
one beside another, each dwindling block
docked like an ocean liner for the dark.

That young man's waiting again
when you enter the estate at night,
stops you politely
with the thinnest echo of a smile,
says *Don't think I'll wait*
till Saturday to slit your throat.
He's gone now, scared you years ago.
No-one shouts your name to come back home.

Climb the stairs: that sandpaper scrape
your shoes make with each step
tattoos your skin. Reach number 45 again
(third storey, red door) but the keys are lost,
your pockets empty.
No-one answers, or whoever answers
never heard of anyone who looks like you.

Rimbaud variations

A dream in winter

This winter we'll ride in a pink carriage
        with blue cushions.
We'll be happy as the wren's song
        whistling from every nook.

Shut your eyes, to shield you from the window
        where evening stretches its jaws
and shadows of running wolves
        smudge the jolting glass.

A scratch will tick your cheek:
this kiss like a panicky spider
races across your neck.

Find it! you'll breathe in my ear.
We'll spend hours hunting that creature
who skitters over your skin.

Sleeper in the valley

That gash in green where the river dreams:
a silver flag flickers from each grass-stalk
as the sun slants down the mountain,
glittering this valley like a lake.

Mouth ajar, head bare, a soldier dozes,
bathing his nape in a puddle of cress.
He lies on green linen, where light dapples him
through the highest cloud.

Ankles steeped in lilies, he naps
with the faintest smile. Cradle him,
Nature, shield him from the cold.

No scent invades him, sleeping in the sun;
his fingers have strayed near his chest,
breast-pocket smeared by two red holes.

5pm in the Green Bar

For a week I scuffed my walking-boots
on the stones of a hundred roads.
At Charleroi I dived in the Green Bar,
ordered beer, a bread door-stop, slab of ham.

Full of myself, I flexed my calves and toes,
traced a gull, a girl on the green tablecloth:
my finger on wings, the line of her lips. It was rich
when that barmaid with nipples big as thimbles

(it'd take more than a kiss to rattle her!)
came laughing with a plate of buttered bread
and slices of warm ham.

Pink ham, its crumbed rind rubbed by a clove
of garlic. When she poured my beer
a tinge of dipping sun foamed gold.

My Bohemia

Fists bunched in pockets, I launched myself,
great-coat flapping like heavenly wings.
I set off to meet the sky, to marry poetry,
or whatever loves dropped crumbs along my path.

That hole in my trousers gaped like a mouth.
Blackberries swung fat rhymes through the hedge
solely for me to pluck and shine and swallow,
as if I'd nick stars from under night's nose.

Those fine September evenings I perched on stones
while shadows speckled dew across my brow,
chilly as one last trickle from the vine.

I rhymed, and tugged my laces
tighter than strings on a lyre,
muddy foot close to my heart.

Evening prayer

Calm as an angel in a barber's chair
clutching a dimpled tankard
I lean back, like I'm offering my throat,
clay-pipe in my teeth, breath filling my sails.

Like hot white shit on a dovecote floor
a thousand dreams singe my insides.
Sap squeezed through my heart's rough bark
simmers from gold to blood.

Once all my dreams are swallowed
I take the air, brimmed by thirty tankards,
ready to set this bitter need free.

Proud as the Lord of the cedar
I piss a sparkling arc towards dark skies,
as if holy water soaks blue heliotropes.

Arsehole sonnet

Puckered as a plum-coloured buttonhole
nestling in moss; the bruise on a mouth
still moist after kisses; the heart of a hem
drawn together by this tightened thread.

A milky ooze
loosens, won't hold back.
It weeps through clots of mottled silt,
lost in snow over slopes.

My dream breathes at the cave-hole;
my jealous soul
warms a nest for its sobbing.

Rapturous as olives, a wheedling flute,
like licking an almond's furrowed skin:
this sip, purple as wine, a promised land.

Vowels

Black A, white E, red I, green U, blue O: vowels.
One day I'll brag your smuggled births.
A's black busk is furred by brilliant flies
dizzy around a stink, this gulf of shadows.

E's a tent of snow, fog breath,
three glacier javelins hurled at winter's kings.
I spits blood; the laugh on lips
from any sorry drunk's a splashed magenta.

U's green ocean circles every coast,
each tide a grassy pasture, jade wrinkles
on a forehead caged by thought.

O the bugle's final note
fades to silence blue as omega,
that violet light caught in my lover's eyes.

Golden dragon

Golden dragon

I sport a gilt quiff,
elaborate as a clarinet
between my brows.

My jaws hinge and unhinge
their glistening umbrella,
my tongue an emperor's belt.

Slide down the S of my neck
and you'll feel drunk from brassy laughter,
hooked by my shark fin wings.

Of course my gold is mottled,
but clouds along serpentine flanks
glint a lizard's blink.

I balance on claws like icicles,
waggle hind legs in tepid air:
a dragon's joie de vivre.

Is my hand-stand not miraculous,
        from my catch-the-light crown
                        to the immaculate
                                    arabesque
                                        of my tail?

The kestrel

Leaning to fill the kettle
near the kitchen window
I see her on the patio
six feet below me.

She must have clocked my shadow,
crouches, waits —
wings like wide autumn-coloured arrows
at their tips; shrewd eye
under a yellow brow;
that head a claw-hammer.

Bunched like a glove in her talons
a fledgling starling
opens and shuts its thin beak.
I think *I have to look*
as she goes about her work,
pausing each couple of seconds
with hunched shoulders to check the air.

Then back to plucking shred by shred,
her weight treading the starling
as if dancing on a cushion.
Breast feathers sputter flecks of ash.
While its narrow beak gapes wide
as if in supplication,
her beak-hook yanks and dips.

It won't die, keeps fidgeting.
She must knead her claws
against its breast,
find the neck and pluck again,
her head swift as hatchet blows

one after another, exposing
pink pincushion skin,
the starling's eye black now,
any glint gone.

She lifts it like a dark stone,
leaves my garden, flaps away.

Failure, my horse

You have to wake up in the middle of the night and hear it…
chomping in the field below, like some loyal horse –
My failure, my very own failure

James Fenton
from *A lesson from Michelangelo*

Failure, my horse,
bridles at fences.
In steeplechases

he prefers to contemplate daisies
or the finely brushed pony-tail
of any rump in front.

He knows precisely where to graze;
gazing at elms,
twitching bluebottles from his ears

he allows a fox to slink
five yards past his flank
over dark fields

sniffing for chickens.
He admires such energy,
but raising one fetlock

before the other
requires art.
To print a hoof exactly,

shaking shadows from the moon
with a shudder of mane,
marks tonight's achievement.

I am horse he thinks,
or stands beyond thinking.
Being horse is sufficient.

Tomorrow
he'll rub his spine
on a satisfying branch,

while chickens peck
elsewhere
and the fox dozes.

Lobster in a Chinese restaurant

Carried on a silver platter
to the table
where three men drink,

one orange strip
neatly clamps each pincer.
The manager tilts her tray,

shows off its size
while the men discuss.
The lobster rears

like an armoured warrior,
its length a mud-green chain.
The blunt fan-tail bends,

abdomen gleaming as seaweed.
Antennae strum the air.
Claws sway like clumsy cutlery

and the men decide.

Pig in the morning

The pig in the morning, when I queue
on the road to work, knows better than me.
She knows the bell-like sway of her saggy
teats as she trots from slop bucket to
gate. Her raised snout sniffs that slack brew:
the swill, the mud, her dung, the scummy
water. It smells like happiness, this simplicity,
though I can't judge. All I know is my view
of her pink and black patched size, her weight,
the stocky dance of her steps by the fence,
the pennants of her ears patting her fat
noble head. So much for my reliance
on wages, work, these wheels, not being late.
Her bum and belly lumber. Her jowls bounce.

The anti-sparrow army

In the early morning the city-wide battle began…Almost half of the labour force was mobilized into the anti-sparrow army…By 8pm tonight it is estimated that a total of 194,432 sparrows have been killed.

Shanghai newspaper, December 1958

They thought they owned the sky,
those dusty mice with wings.
We proved otherwise.

Every hour through invaded air
we clattered pans, ladles, lids.
That racket became our music.

We dared not let them settle
wiry claws
on any branch.

Wings drooped, a feeble beating,
until they dropped,
brown hailstones from a cloud.

Contemplate the silence.
No beaks.
No cheap bickering.

If the sky sizzles later with locusts
we'll forbid them. The sky
will hear our words and must obey.

Esther Phillips and the python

On the seventies album cover
     her smile is wary, her gaze taut
above the python's lips. She holds him
     like a dangerous saxophone
in her manicured nails,
     the tapered leaf of his delicate head
a mouthpiece she won't blow.

     The full-stop of his eye
opens. Thick paprika diamonds
     slink along what might be air-holes
if he could be played; his underbelly
     a muscled rope striped by ash smudges,
his body her wavering testament:
     slippery song, this slithered hallelujah.

The last fly of winter

The last fly of winter's out of season —
uselessly fussing against glass,
wanting sun to polish each wing,
to gorge once more on the turds of summer,
alight on dropped ice-creams,
dizzy and sick on a hare's liver
squashed in the road
to glory as the facets of its eyes glitter
with black promises of heat, more heat —
to sip this endless feast — scorched desire
dwindling now through the milkiest morning,
slowing its legs across a chill windowsill,
parched as a leaf and alone.

The next word
for Ann Atkinson

When the right hand raises its pen
the tongue sings a hundred linnets,
as if a beak nips each finger.

One phrase chains another —
the caterpillar slinks across a leaf,
the crocodile blinks once in warm shallows.

Steer into this skid — ice splitting
under a skater's heel, sun hatching
between branches, woken by a peacock's yelp.

Arrive at this journeying wrist,
the next word about to be written:
hare-print on a fog-blurred page.

Husbands

In Justice Square

for Mahmoud Asgari and Ayaz Marhoni, aged 17 and 18,
publicly hanged in Justice Square, Mashhad, Iran on July 19 2005,*
for allegedly conducting homosexual acts

When my hand, palm down on the table,
rested, waited, for a chance that his smallest finger
might touch mine momentarily,
my wish was granted and my heart
flew from its cage.

When his eyes looked at mine for seconds longer
than was necessary, and my gaze
strayed to his mouth like a bee to hibiscus,
this was forbidden:
each finger, that minute, my eyes, his mouth
unlawful.

If we knew our skin to be lovesick
why risk the thought of a kiss?
The prospect of his breath an inch from mine
shook my nights. His voice spoke of danger,
shame and fear while I watched his lips
shape the words, his tongue
sing each sentence.

The slope of his shoulders became my prayer.
I can't sleep in their mercy now,
more secretive than murmurs.
Boys do it until weddings beckon.
Would we both have obeyed our fathers
to become good men?
When they lash my back I'll confess anything,
waking again to the smell of blood.

Let us be an example.
Break our hands and we'll repent our sin.
Cut the noose and we'll deny each other,
renounce all men from this day forward,
as if the blindfolds knotted round our eyes
stay bound tight and are never undone.

Moment

You stroked his arm, quietly said *He's gone.*
I knew the air had dimmed because
he no longer breathed in it.
By walking and speaking
he altered the colour of words,
made each room he moved in
a space I wanted to share: now
this secluded ward that held four of us,
until you quietly said *He's gone,*
shattered three of us, except of course
it still bore his weight on the sheet
in the centre of the room, as though
his bed had become the world's axis.

His bed had become the world's axis
in the centre of the room, as though
it still bore his weight on the sheet,
shattered three of us, except of course
until you quietly said *He's gone.*
This secluded ward that held four of us
(a space I wanted to share now)
made each room he moved in.
He altered the colour of words
by walking and speaking.
He no longer breathed in it.
I knew the air had dimmed because
you stroked his arm, quietly said *He's gone.*

Last night

When you said *I love you* in my dream
you were already dead. I grabbed my chance
to return the compliment. The last time
you were here, palpably here, to glance
or laugh or walk into a room,
kissing my cheek as your shy hello,
was twenty years ago. It should bring gloom
to count those years, so why this secret glow
that half a life later I welcome you
in dreams? I love our achievement.
Your hand still touches my skin; the echo
of your voice reverberates in my throat.
Bastard death can do its worst, wipe you away,
but last night you were here again, to stay.

Crash

Does death interrupt like this? No preparation.
Headlights flood our faces; the smash hard enough
to shake mauve roses through our skin.
A singed, smoky smell. Air-bags sag their rough
creased clouds in silence when I ask
Are you allright? You have to be.
When you answer we stumble for the dark,
shouts and shadows, breeze, a creaky tree.
I wake and sleep, you wake and sleep.
Headlights stun our windscreen.
We're back in the moment, running a tape
that might have finished us, didn't, a spin
of tyres, the second before your voice
answers everything and I touch your face.

Late

You were late and suddenly the world spun
without you while I stood alone in it,
waiting outside the shop for a man
who wouldn't come, as every stone minute
clattered down the street. I checked the time.
You were later than magnolias in July,
cherries in autumn. Perhaps a crime
stopped you, or your heart snatched you away.
I ransacked my head for reasons. It felt like
the hour before I knew you, only lonelier.
Since your fingers sparked the strike
of flames across my skin, what's holier
than that? What's more welcome than seeing
your face in a crowd, with blackbirds singing?

A letter to Helen

You aren't losing a battle with cancer.
I think you're bowing to the body's dangerous
miracles with humility, with reverence.
When you say *I'm dying* you don't mean
this afternoon, this hour.

Where does love carry me, animal of change?
To a nursing home garden
where I splinter the rosemary between
fingers and thumb, for you
to breathe its scent.

Bloom longer than the orchids on your sill.
In this narrowing room
two old friends talk honestly again
and I can't comprehend you'll go.

I kissed a stone and skimmed it over waves
the day you died, as if signing myself on water —
always yours.

Postscript

It's been three months. Can you come back
now please? We haven't finished
our conversation. There's more I need to say,
even more to hear, especially your voice
again, that saucy laugh, and could
I listen to your bossiness? I miss it:
all those decisive opinions in a café
or your kitchen. What a fool I was
not to fall on my knees and thank you
for every talk, phone call, text.
Yes I've saved the last seven, and open
them on my screen again, as if they
might be the smallest whisper of your
next word last word next word last word next.

Tomorrow

This face you find in the mirror
alters again, imperceptibly.
Trust me: the eyes stay the same.

Rooms become a road
trod morning to evening, the path to the kitchen,
your fingers trailing a banister,
that bed another milestone
welcome as a dent in the pillow.

Dear warrior, you can withstand the years,
even waltz with them.
Run through the garden at night
as the moon fills its bowl of milk again
and your path is crossed by snails.

Thanking the house

Place your palm like a quiet blessing
on the nearest wall, familiar as your skin,

while the blossom tree outside
flickers its snow towards morning

and that puddle forms a map of Australia
drop by drop.

Doors sing on their hinges
for your bright guests to enter:

for the kids to ease off their trainers,
crash across the settee,

for your face in the blurred mirror
to feature a cloud, dispersing

through your garden, that room of roses,
where ringdoves jab at sunflower seeds.

Becoming a Lucian Freud nude

Scratching my elbow, I glance in the long
bathroom mirror. Time has smudged its thumb
on sags and jowls:
                    drooping fruit,
as if extra flesh on a waistline
         signifies defeat
in the face of jogs or swims.

Follow the forehead into middle age,
these seams across skin.
Suppose linen can't be smoothed again —
         all my ripples counted,
though I've earned them, even the neck's
fine creases. What miracles
are moving here, what transformation?

Travel down the shoulders to the breasts,
my mottled nipples, where sparse hairs cluster
and the heart hides.
                    I see few ribs,
         contemplate my navel:
its dint of shadow, the belly's comma,
above a disappointed penis.

Blotches, moles and blemishes
         map my years
in coral, oyster, pink, reddening
my thighs that suffer cream twice daily.
Do my knees disagree with each other?
         Mark how vulnerably
their knots and nodules coincide.

Brushstrokes prickle each ankle
through ageing light;
                 the finale of feet.
Naked as day, my body should speak.
          What shapes its song?
Victory's here — from stubble to shin,
from hip to wrist to temple.

Husbands

We say vows in a roomful of friends.
A new ring circles my finger.
Now we think of ourselves as husbands,
speak the secret at night to each other.
Husband – a language of echoes for me,
having loosened the ropes from that name
before we met. Might it set us free?
Could we live in this title like a home
with its glass roof and windows,
or is the word a coracle, tilting the weight
of both syllables, balanced by shadows,
dipping oars with a coastline in sight?
Two men stroll arm in arm along the shore
buttoned like husbands, brimful, wanting more.

Being the sea

Being the sea

This morning
gulls float on my skin like a hand
across a forehead, the skim of it
feeling my chill, my fever.

One wave cuffs another like heartbeats,
eardrum pulsing whenever I dream.
Fish spurt through me in glittery shoals,
nets half-empty on a late afternoon
although a shark still hangs by my quayside,
the suede of its fin stroking my fingers.

My edge casts a handful of pebbles
an inch from your ankle.
My tide shoves rocky heaves
hard against crashed weather.
Hours sway past turquoise to gun-metal,
peach to flamingo when the sun gives up.

Scrunch your heels beside my ebb.
Listen tonight at last for my hiss:
nearly a promise, almost a threat
in the moon's white dazzle over black shallows,
my cloak of oceans, my marvellous deep.

Nesting

No baby this time. We're nesting for ourselves.
In the same way as we've chosen to move
to the sea, we can decide which shelves
that bowl, those books and tulips might crave
if we were them: to fit, perhaps belong.
Move them again, until we've found
the right spot, while the sun slides its oblong
mirror across a rug and each new sound
in the flat creaks or clicks its music.
We're rooting in this soil like two bare trees
about to blossom, every petal a fleck
outside the window, rising as we please,
nodding to neighbours. Take my hand.
We could even call it home: here, where we stand.

Unpacking the books

They're in alphabetical order.
What better democracy?
A birdsong of Clares, rainbow of Dotys,
sextet of Gunns — paper companions
establish me through unfamiliar rooms.

I wedge my handful of pamphlets,
my own narrow volumes,
between Hacker and Hamilton. My name
tiptoes down three spines.

Will I fit here, picked from a shelf,
skimmed or discarded?
I've been told there's no competition
but hardly believe it.

A swarm of Plaths, the searchlights of Rich,
voices from a sharper conversation
I step into and aim to translate.
Who spells another language I'm greedy to hear?

Drunk on someone else's lines
I forget my new address, open books
to discover my absence, speak a phrase
for burnished pages, a word that means alone.

35C

If I know that mould may blossom from you,
that water may seep between floorboards
one soggy morning, I should forbid myself,
and yet, the curve of your shoulder
(I mean your wall) makes me a young man
in love again, no — face it, an older man
for the seventh time in love with a house,
this time not even a house,
our portion of it, six rooms below stairs,
where legs walk higher than my forehead
and passing eyes glance through our windows,
reading scrolls and swirls on the rug, its fanfares,
noting acorns and oak-leaves on our cushions,
the faces caught by our history
smiling from shelves, names down the spines,
cellos of grain on the doors, brass handles.

If I tread across carpets through chill dark,
avoiding the cat silent as fog
in a subtle lime sheen from the smoke alarm,
I'll reach my other love between sheets,
where fear of him disappearing
mixes with wonder at him staying.
Is this the same swoon? The curve of your wall
(I mean your shoulder) the gate of your songs
(I mean your rooms) the map of your coasts
(I mean your ceilings) the rose of your moon
(I mean your rose). Do we build a marriage
from each other, commit ourselves to cornices,
key-holes and dado-rails, to skirting-boards,
thresholds and curtains, veiny white tiles
and daffodil bulbs rising like
manicured green fingernails from good soil?

Sunday

A young man's angel wings
tattooed on his shoulder blades
feather either side of his spine.

Where does my son go
when he speaks in tongues?
I worry for him. I want to call him back.

The Big Issue seller says urgently
I need something to eat
as if he could haunt me with words.

That time in Paris, stifling your cries
with kisses
so they shook inside my mouth.

After lunch we walk to the sea.
I hunt poetry books that aren't there,
read Fuck Off on a punk girl's scalp.

When it rains briefly we unfurl umbrellas.
Yours rests later in the bath,
open as a black sunflower.

Tonight's clarinettist coils smoky jazz.
His path snakes through the loops,
the spools and swoons, always returning.

I'm speaking in tongues to a black sunflower
homeless with hunger, naked as Paris,
a stone thrown in broken water
for the length of a clarinettist's breath.

Bette Davis on Brighton pier

Bette is sick of Hollywood.
The chauffeur's tucked up for the night.
Blurred by cigarette smoke
wrapped in her slinkiest fur,
woozy from one too many dry martinis
she wants to walk on the pier
risking her stilettos.

The moon won't be star-struck
as she sashays in her burgundy
satin off-the-shoulder number
from the party in *All About Eve*.
The fans don't know her anymore.
She's years out of date,
stalking like a sulky duchess along the planks.

Past doughnut stalls, guzzling gulls,
the penny falls and shooting games;
past child-sized cranes letting Homer Simpson
slip through their silver clutches;
past lasers, car chases, change machines;
past Moo Moo's, hundreds of flavours,
the best shakes in town.

She wants horses, their carousel dazzling
the dark; their rosettes and florid swirls.
Climbing up among mirrors and light-bulbs
she wants to gallop on golden hooves,
the hurdy-gurdy whirling her
as she swoops towards the sea,
riding those cold black waves,
breathing their manes and swerves,
unfastening her seat-belt for another bumpy night.

Leaving the party early

My dead friend said *Why not leave*
the party early? So, on the stroke
of midnight, before I become a pumpkin
or mouse, without dropping a glass
slipper, I abandon the songs I barely know,
and hear – through open windows higher
than myself – *Dancing Queen*, where
I'd been a dancing queen ten minutes
ago. The freedom of walking away,
dodging the cars when lights are green.
I eat a kebab, me – a vegetarian
for thirty years – with no-one telling me
not to, thinking *I'll dance for as long*
as I choose, and never leave.

Shoelaces

Untying shoelaces late at night
I think this is how people live:
untying our laces, drinking with friends,
running on a wheel, fretting and laughing,
dipping our heads under a lilac branch
as it leans over a fence into the street,
hearing a blackbird on an aerial
welcome the evening, knowing we'll never know
when time will take us, but it will,
the lilac, the blackbird, the shoelaces
always unravelling, infinitely precious,
the moment we sit on the edge
of our beds, late at night, after a drink
with friends, thinking this is how people live.

My husband sleeping

Resting my hand on you means you're here.
Your bent elbow, that tender pyramid,
troubles the sheet while you breathe. A brief snore
slackens your mouth. In sleep you turn your head
so I'm sensing your face through the dark,
relaxed and unaware, inches from mine
on our separate pillows. If I kiss your neck
and keep myself this near I'll catch your moan
or laugh inside a dream, where I can't reach,
though we're close as tongues, secret as skin.
Lying together night after night could teach
lovers about each other, if one
or both were awake enough to hear
a hand touching a man, finger by finger.

At Coleton Fishacre

You tell me to go ahead without you,
through gardens where a path dips steeply
to the sea. You say you'll wait for me.
We remember your heart, and the view
from this coast is nothing compared to
recovery: what once seemed easy
might be breathless now. I should walk freely
down the slope, alone, to stroke a blue
hydrangea, to shudder the bells of that
fuchsia with my fingers. Is this what I want?
The gardens look insufficient without
you. Come with me; although I know you can't,
at least not today. So I study the white
of tall daisies, note how the foxgloves slant.

Funeral tie

for Suzie, Annie, Laurie, Nettie and Hannah

Silky liquorice, I take you out
too often these days, for an aunt,
a mother, an uncle, two more aunts.

They were the grown-ups:
standing stones; with us,
the small ones, encircled.

What ties does a tie understand?
Years happened.
I loop, knot and pinch you again.

Black as a labrador's tail
you flap in the breeze
when we circle an open grave.

I notice my cousin's ear
has become a middle-aged ear.
What alchemy lengthened our lobes?

You'd like to fly
                    above the relatives,
loosen a charcoal signature
        among the clouds.

The AIDS memorial
for Clifford and Andrew

Will you write our story? Do you want me to? You have to he said
no-one but you can write it.

Patti Smith
from *Just Kids*

1.

    Two bronze men in verdigris
    unfurl from each other,
    as if a red ribbon's twist
    crosses below their thighs,
    their armless torsos, buffeted chests,
    risen throats naked to the sky.

    It's ancient history. We've got it licked.
    No-one dies here; all those dazzling fairies
    dated as neat moustaches and Bronski Beat.

    I circle this turmoil
    within the sea's sight:
    two flown men caught.
    Can I cast this net to haul you back?
    Twenty years and nine years dead,
    should I leave you in peace
    or leave myself twice bereft?

    Twenty years —
    staccato as breathing, harsh
    as recalling with no-one to listen.

2.

Clifford
where's the triumph in such recollection?
Didn't we finish this conversation
a lifetime ago? It started with your name.

We sat, two diffident eleven-year-olds
at joined desks. Bitten pencils,
dog-eared books, chewed-up spat-out paper globs
whizzed around us, missing their mark
in the chaos when the teacher left our class.
What makes two boys catch each other's message?
I wanted to hear whatever you said next.

Where's the teenage tape we made
of *The Waste Land* ? Me singing,
you plink-plonking your secondhand red piano.
Arias and diminuendos
bloom before they dwindle into air.

You're on the brink
of Art College, telling me you're gay.
I never guessed: often a lag behind,
sometimes missing your point.

Then I'm married, preoccupied.
You sway in a chair bought to lull
our first baby, saying into silence
I've got AIDS, correct yourself: *HIV.*

You and Andrew built your lives
as if glass might carry the sky.
Your brush, a thistle or fuchsia,
stippled each canvas.

Snail-shells and pylons,
cooling towers, peacocks and gasworks,
lily-pads, light-bulbs and half-moons
blaze from your farewell, celebrate
today across my walls. I rise to them
every morning. They sing your name.

Occasionally in dreams you're well again,
your skinny diminuendo etched through me.
Once I lifted my toddler son
to your hospital window, where you waved
at each other. He had chickenpox, you shingles,
although I can't remember how we were
protecting you, or thought we were.

The last time we spoke
I kissed your knuckles when you thanked me,
as though you'd become a prince.
The feather-breath you finished
before Andrew said *He's gone*
led me weeping to the sheet
between your head and stopped shoulder.

Andrew twists roses through your wreath
My Funny Valentine and I recite Hopkins
at your funeral, stilled to a crowded hush.
My breath hovered until *My own heart*
let me more have pity on. The son I lifted
to your window has forgotten you.
These surging verdigris men
swirl from each other.
I relinquish ash blown towards the tide.

3.

Andrew
where's the rescue from such memories?
They smack like waves, relentless
in the plunge, this blur of blue
agapanthus with creamy Russian vine.

Two bereft friends cling to each other,
as the drunks beside this memorial
slur stories to fill their hours.
When thirty balloon-strings
loosen through our fingers, a mother shouts
her son's name at the clouds, over and over,
as if one repeated word might voice her loss.

Thank you for making that T-Shirt:
I'M POSITIVE...LIFE IS WONDERFUL
in black capitals across your chest,
for shoppers and browsers to read
your body's message. You taught me
to pluck happiness like a harebell
from the nettles. Teach me now.

Thank you for saying *Why not*
leave the party early? as if
foreseeing the brief violet
of your death.

You fell in the market
among lettuces and gooseberries,
sugar-cane, okra and barrow-boy yells.
Halfway through your organised day,
buying CDs, walking back to your flat,
a shut heart, the pavement's pillow.

I enter the ward twenty years ago,
find you quietly lying together,
this glade of calm, my breath an intrusion.
Forgive me. I should rewrite my arrival,
win you an hour's blessing in his arms.

After such friends, how to continue?
It's ancient history, forever circling
two verdigris men who strive
beyond grass like silver birches.

Tonight your names
join a list at the service.
Couples and singles cup their flames
by this floodlit memorial.
Once I'm numb from too much snow
I'll kneel before the sea's crashed gardenias.

Blue wallpaper

The boats on my bedroom wallpaper
entered my days.
I read each yacht-sail with a finger:
their wind-billows, their cream triangles
made my bed a steady hull.

Now I walk by the sea, having found it,
as years before I left my mother and aunt
on the sand, strolled with my uncle,
brother and cousin to meet the waves.

The tide stayed out then
and wouldn't seep back for hours.
We passed men and boys digging
for lugworms in pleated sand.

That wide afternoon
over ribbed puddles, a wet beach oozy
under our footprints, the sea glimmered
its crinkle of tinfoil along the horizon.

Today, out in the air, I reach
the top of my steps and look ahead,
where twenty yacht-sails sharp as cuttlefish
flick across waves.

I'm here and a hundred miles away;
this morning and fifty years ago
roll together, swayed in the hull,
like light strumming water over and over.

Without blue wallpaper
or my mother, without my children
holding my hands, I stand
at the prow of my house, a boat on the sea.